# Tate Modern
# **The Building**

## A new gallery for modern art

The Tate Gallery started life at Millbank on the north bank of the Thames, and was originally known as the 'National Gallery of British Art'. The first visitors to cross its neo-classical threshold in 1897 could examine 245 paintings – many gifted to the nation by sugar magnate Henry Tate, along with the gallery itself – displayed in just eight rooms. In 1917 Tate was officially given responsibility for housing the nation's modern international collection as well as British works, and for the next eighty-three years the collections were exhibited side-by-side within the gallery at Millbank.

Despite a series of building extensions over the subsequent decades, by the late 1980s it became clear that the collection had outgrown its home at Millbank and a new gallery was a matter of urgency. The creation of a separate site for the modern international works would mean more exhibition space and stronger separate identities of the two collections. It was decided to create a new gallery in London to display the international modern component of the Tate collection. For the first time London would have a dedicated museum of modern art. At the same time, the Tate building on Millbank would neatly revert to its original intended function as the national gallery of British art from 1500 onwards, changing from the Tate Gallery to Tate Britain.

In December 1992 a press conference was held to announce plans to create a new Tate Gallery of Modern Art and the hunt began for an appropriate site.

## Choosing a site

An immediate problem was whether the modern art gallery should be a new building or a conversion of an existing building, if a suitable one could be found. As a result of extensive consultations, particularly with artists, it was decided to search for a building to convert. Several locations within central London were assessed: the South Bank, Effra (near Vauxhall), Greenwich Reach and Bankside Power Station were all considered.

The Bankside Power Station was an exciting possibility but seemed impossibly large. Director Nicholas Serota visited the building one evening on his way home from work, and set about roughly calculating its size by pacing the length and width of it and counting his steps. He estimated that the footprint was in fact approximately the same as the Gallery at Millbank – thus its apparently daunting scale seemed much more manageable. When the Trustees visited the building in July 1993 they were overwhelmed; it was in an amazing location on the south bank of the River Thames opposite St Paul's Cathedral and the City of London. The fact that the original Tate Gallery was also on the river made for a satisfactory symmetry, and meant that the two could be linked by a riverboat service. And the power station was a striking and distinguished building in its own right, designed by Sir Giles Gilbert Scott, architect of Battersea Power Station and Waterloo Bridge, and the designer of the famous British red telephone box. In April 1994 Bankside Power Station was formally announced as the chosen site to house The Tate Gallery of Modern Art.

**Left**
**Aerial view of Bankside Power Station in the foreground, looking across the Thames to St Paul's Cathedral, 1991.**

**Right**
**Tate Modern at twilight, 1999.**

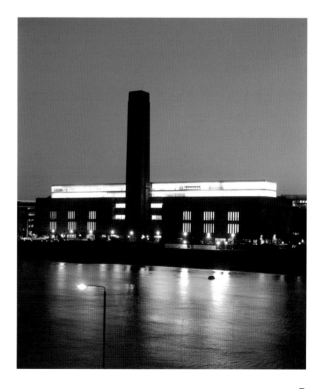

## The power station

Built in two phases between 1947 and 1963, Bankside Power Station was conceived by Giles Gilbert Scott as a new kind of cathedral, a cathedral of pure energy. However, Gibert Scott – who also designed several churches and came from a line of ecclesiastical architects – intentionally made the power station chimney shorter than the Dome of St Paul's Cathedral across the river.

The western half of the structure, which included the chimney, replaced an earlier coal-fired power station in 1952. The eastern half of the building was brought into commission in 1963. Inevitably technological change meant that the power station gradually slipped into obsolescence. In 1981 it closed due to increased oil prices, making other methods of generating electricity more efficient. Between 1981 and 1994, when the Tate Gallery acquired an option on the site, the building remained unoccupied apart from an operational London Electricity sub-station, which continues to function alongside the gallery.

## From power station to gallery

Tate held an international competition to select the architect who would transform the industrial building into a gallery. Over seventy architects entered, including some of the world's most distinguished. The final choice, announced in January 1995, was Herzog & de Meuron, a relatively small and then little-known Swiss firm. The dignified simplicity of their proposal impressed the jury. Their respect for the original architecture, with subtle alterations rather than grand gestures, and the introduction of more light via the enormous roof light box, combined to create an interior both functional and modern. A key factor in this choice was that their proposal retained much of the essential character of the building. One of the shortlisted architects had, for example, proposed demolishing the ninety-nine metre high chimney, a central feature of the building.

In March 1996, Herzog & de Meuron's designs for the Tate Gallery of Modern Art were unveiled in full, and two months later a grant of £12 million was made to Tate by national regeneration agency English Partnerships, enabling the acquisition of the Bankside site. In December the architects opened an office at the site to oversee the building work.

In order to begin the transformation of Bankside Power Station into an art gallery, the site had to be cleared and prepared for rebuilding. The structure consisted of a vast Turbine Hall, thirty-five metres high and one hundred and fifty-five metres long, with the boiler house alongside it. All the machinery of the Turbine Hall was removed and a number of outbuildings demolished, leaving the building stripped back to its original steel and brickwork. The Turbine Hall became a dramatic entrance area, with ramped access from the west and as a display space for large sculptural projects and commissions. The architects celebrated its industrial vernacular by leaving steel columns exposed and by retaining a monument to engineering – two huge gantry cranes, capable of carrying up to seventy tons.

**Bankside Power Station Turbine Hall, 1994, before the turbines were removed.**

The boiler house became home to galleries on three levels running the full length of the building for displays from the permanent collection and temporary exhibitions. Above the original roofline of the power station Herzog & de Meuron added a two-storey glass penthouse, known as the lightbeam. By day this area affords spectacular views of the river and the City; after dark it is illuminated, marking the presence of Tate Modern for miles around.

Construction work on Tate Modern was completed in late 1999, and in January 2000 artworks began to be installed in the galleries. Following the launch of Tate Britain in March, Tate Modern was officially opened by Queen Elizabeth II on 11 May 2000, (the queen had also presided over the opening of the Bankside Power Station, some thirty-seven years earlier).

### The first decade
Over its first ten years, Tate Modern firmly established itself as one of the UK's top three tourist attractions, generating an estimated £100m in economic benefits to London annually. Its firm position in the national – and international – consciousness can be seen as the result of the synthesis between its collection, its dynamic programme of temporary exhibitions and events and the way all of these inhabit the dramatically varied spaces within the building. The Turbine Hall lies somewhere between an outdoor public space and a conventional gallery and has presented a unique platform for sculpture and new kinds of exhibition. A series of annual artist commissions, supported by Unilever, has provided the opportunity for contemporary artists to make site-specific works in response to the spatial, historic or social resonances of the Hall. It is also a vast public arena for a range of media including dance, performance, film and video. The broad spectrum of exhibitions shown within the more traditional gallery spaces has encompassed major retrospectives of modern masters and surveys of important movements and tendencies in art. Medium-scale shows provide an opportunity to focus on one aspect of an artist's oeuvre, or to make a mid-career celebration of a living artist. Project spaces have enabled Tate Modern to be a laboratory for the new, providing young artists with a place for experimentation.

### The Tate Modern Project
Tate Modern's popularity has far exceeded expectations. Designed for an annual audience of two million, it now receives four and a half million visitors each year, making it the world's most visited museum of modern art. This success has put pressure on existing facilities and programme. Though Tate Modern has more than twice the number of visitors as MoMA in New York or the Centre Pompidou in Paris, it has about half the gallery space. The breadth of Tate Modern's audience is continuing to develop in response to its programmes and outreach work. More space is needed to welcome people, and different kinds of gallery are needed to better display the works in the collection.

Film, video, photography and performance have become more essential strands of artistic practice, and artists have

**The Turbine Hall after removal of the old machinery, 1997.**

embraced new technologies. Ambitious and imaginative installations are now pushing traditional gallery spaces to their limits, as reflected in Tate's acquisitions. When Tate Modern opened there were eighty-six large-scale installations in the collection; now there are more than three hundred. With these developments in mind, in 2009 Tate embarked on a major project to extend Tate Modern, working again with architects Herzog & de Meuron. The transformed Tate Modern will make use of the power station's spectacular redundant oil tanks, increase gallery space by sixty per cent, and provide much improved visitor facilities.

The expansion will create a less congested, more welcoming environment. The exhibition and display space will be almost doubled, putting much more of the Tate collection on show. Learning will be at the heart of the new Tate Modern, reflecting Tate's commitment to increasing public knowledge and understanding of art. There will be a range of new facilities throughout the building promoting deeper engagement with art: interpretation, discussion, private study, participation, workshops and practice based learning. The ambition is to redefine the museum for the twenty-first century, placing artists and their art at Tate Modern's centre while fully integrating the display, learning and social functions of the museum, and strengthening links between the museum, its community and the city.

### An ideal opportunity to expand
The opening of Tate Modern in 2000 was intended as the first stage in the development of the former Bankside Power Station. It was always envisaged that the derelict oil tanks and the switch station to the south of the site could eventually be integrated into the gallery.

The electrical switch station is still used to power a large part of the City and South London. UKPN, formerly EDF, who own the station, have modernised their equipment so that it takes up a smaller part of the building, freeing up more than 1,000 square metres of space for the expansion. This provides us with the ideal opportunity to expand Tate Modern, with the oil tanks forming the foundation of the new building. Like the original Tate Modern, the new building is designed by Herzog & de Meuron and will present a striking combination of the raw and the refined, found industrial spaces and twenty-first-century architecture.

### Switch station and oil tanks
If the Turbine Hall was the defining emblem of Tate Modern's first stage, the vast oil tanks, at the base of the building, will become as closely associated with the new building. These raw industrial spaces will retain their rough-edged atmosphere to become a unique setting for artists' installations and performances, including dance, music, the spoken word and film. Tank 1 will be programmed with changing displays, exhibitions and radical commissions of contemporary art. Tank 2 will be used for performances and events, complementing the display programme in Tank 1. Supporting facilities such as green rooms will be located in Tank 3. Three new galleries will also be created from raw 'as-found' spaces adjacent

to the tanks which originally contained Bankside Power Station's ancillary plant and equipment.

Taken together, the tanks and 'as-found' galleries will place the exploration of contemporary visual art practice, and its resonance in performance and contemporary thought, at the foundation of the transformed Tate Modern.

### The new building
Rising from the tanks, beautiful new galleries displaying the collection will have a greater variation of sizes and shapes than the original museum, and there will be a larger space for temporary exhibitions, new seminar spaces and a cutting-edge media lab. Social spaces will include a new Members' Room, a Level 9 restaurant, and a public terrace on Level 10 all with outstanding views across the capital.

The façade will use brick to match the surface of the existing Tate Modern building, while creating something radically new – a perforated brick lattice through which the interior lights will glow in the evening. Windows and the terrace will appear as cuts in the brick surface. The building will rise 64.5 metres above ground in eleven levels, its height responding to the iconic chimney of Giles Gilbert Scott's power station, which is itself a response to the dome of St Paul's across the river.

### Sustainability
The new building will be a model of environmental sustainability, drawing much of its energy needs from heat emitted by UKPN's transformers in the adjoining operational switch house. With a high thermal mass, use of natural ventilation and daylight, the new structure will use 54 per cent less energy and generate 44 per cent less carbon than current building regulations demand.

### Closer to the community
There will be two new public squares to the south and west of the building. To the east, a new planted area will be created especially for the use of the local community and staff. Tate Modern is part of the neighbourhood. Its presence has made a major contribution to the ongoing revitalisation of Southwark, and it recognises the importance of building strong links with the local community. The Transforming Tate Modern project will be a catalyst for engaging local audiences more deeply and broadening access to the museum.

The new development will continue to bolster the growth of the borough. A public walkway through the building will make possible a direct route from the City to the heart of Southwark. Opening up new ways for people to navigate their way through London is just one example of how the transformed Tate Modern will be a radical realisation of the museum as a shared public space.

**The architects' vision for (left) the Tanks, and (right) the new building.**

Left
View from the north bank of the
Thames, 2010.

Overleaf
Panorama from the west.

Michael Craig-Martin's *Swiss Light* 1999, on top of the chimney, was a temporary enhancement in collaboration with Herzog & de Meuron, symbolising the birth of the Gallery and the reincarnation of Bankside. It was dismantled in 2008.

Above
The glass roof above the
Turbine Hall.

Right
View from the west in 2001.

The light display at the opening on 11 May 2000.

TATE MODERN: COLLECTION 2000

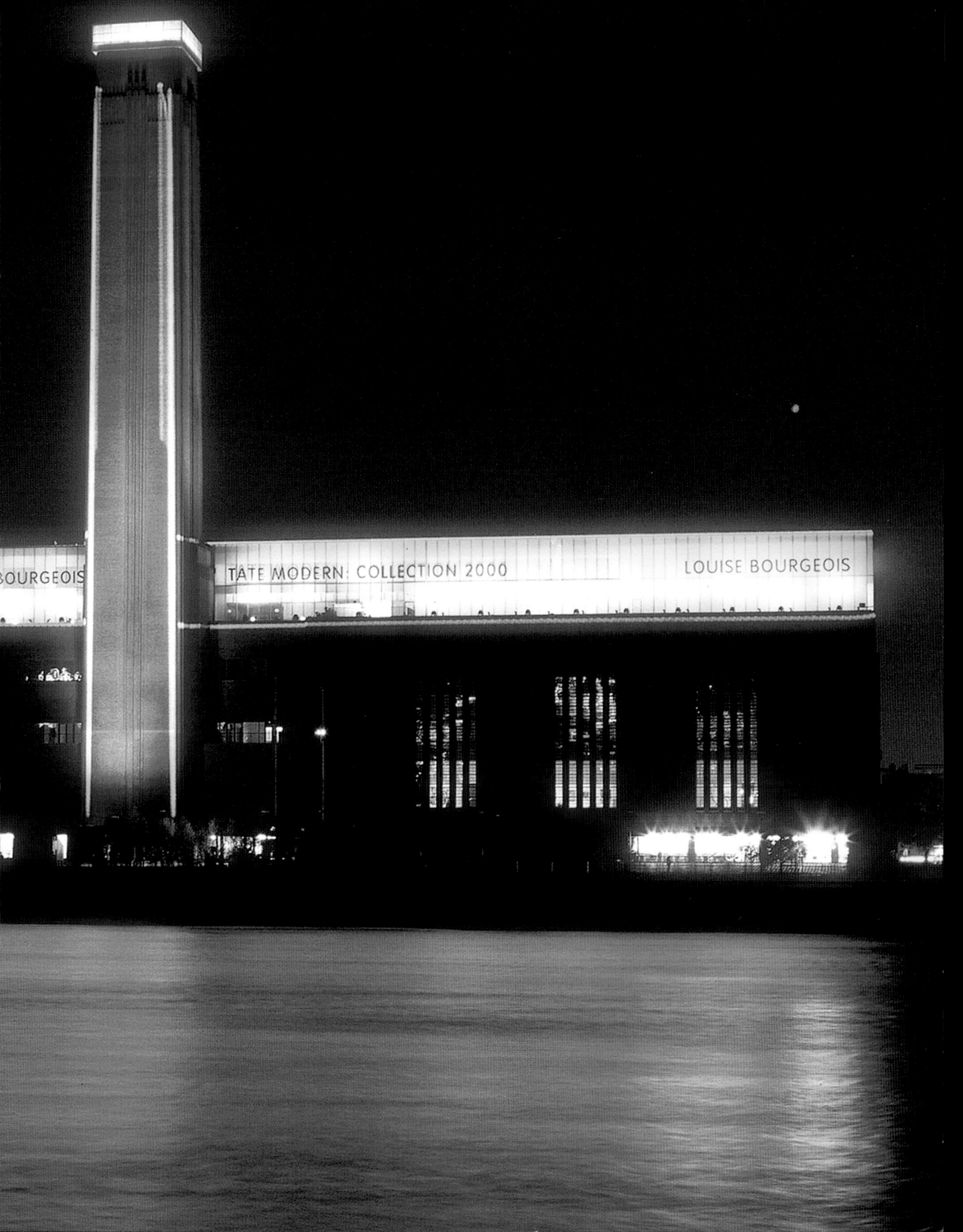
BOURGEOIS
TATE MODERN: COLLECTION 2000
LOUISE BOURGEOIS

Louise Bourgeois's *I Do, I Undo, I Redo* 2000 (above) and *Maman* 1999 (right), were cast for the first of The Unilever Series of works commissioned annually for the Turbine Hall between 2000 and 2012.

Carsten Höller's *Test Site* 2006
(above) and Olafur Eliasson's
*The Weather Project* 2003 (right),
both commissioned for The
Unilever Series.

**Above**
Do Ho Suh's *Staircase-III* 2010.

**Right**
The double-height gallery on
Level 2, showing Joseph Beuys's
*Lightning with Stag in its Glare*
1958–85.

Above
The view through the galleries
on Level 2.

Right
Ai Weiwei's *Sunflower Seeds*
2010, The Unilever Series.

Jenny Holzer's *BLUE PURPLE TILT* 2007 on Level 4.

MY ROOM HAS FOUR DOORS NOT
MY ROOM HAS FOUR DOORS NOT
MY ROOM HAS FOUR DOORS NOT
MY ROOM HAS FOUR DOORS NOT
MY ROOM HAS FOUR DOORS NOT
MY ROOM HAS FOUR DOORS NOT

Above
Doris Salcedo's *Shibboleth* 2007,
The Unilever Series.

Right
Anish Kapoor's Unilever Series
commission, *Marsyas* 2002.
Above the work is one of the two
gantry cranes preserved from
the original power station, and
still used today for installing and
dismantling works of art in the
Turbine Hall.

Previous page
The Rothko Room on Level 2.

Right
Tacita Dean's Unilever Series
commission, *FILM* 2011.

Previous page
The restaurant on Level 6, looking out across the river to St Paul's Cathedral.

Left
*Street Art* 2008, the first commission to use the river façade to display work. The six artists are Blu, the collective Faile, JR, Nunca, Os Gemeos, and Sixeart.

# Conversation
## Nicholas Serota and Jacques Herzog

**Nicholas Serota** The choice of the site was motivated by two considerations. One was what we thought Bankside would yield as a space to show art. But the choice of location was undoubtedly engendered in part by the recognition that creating a great museum of modern art in the centre of a city does create a public space and a public attraction. Britain is not organised in the way France is organised. It is not a great public project, an initiative by government. It is an initiative taken by a small group of people whose powers are limited, but one of the powers that we did have was to try and put it on a site where it would have a public presence and in a part of the city where its arrival would make a difference.

**Jacques Herzog** The very ingenious thing in terms of urbanism that you and only you saw was that Bankside was an incredible chance, which for some unbelievable reason was not discovered before. Now everybody understands. The choice of Bankside was almost an act of urbanism to which we as architects didn't contribute anything. The only thing we could then contribute was trying to understand what the location is and to try to develop it very logically according to connecting paths and lines, the river, the bridge, the situation with St Paul's. We conceived the building as something permeable, something you walk through, and as something that literally attracts people, a public plaza. And the turbine hall was the obvious place to make that connection between the outside and the inside, the galleries, the people, the art – and everything comes from that idea.

**NS** Herzog & de Meuron realised that the turbine hall

**Left**
The west façade.

**Right**
The view of Tate Modern from
St Paul's Cathedral in 2003.

was essentially a street that ran through the building and that it had both a north façade and a south façade. But the bold move on the turbine hall was to take out the decking that formed a floor at ground level. It was bold because it meant that we were losing the possibility of creating a basement space below that floor, that is to say giving up a huge volume where conventionally people might have put an auditorium or a black box space or whatever. The benefit of giving it up was that as the visitor comes down to that lowest level they see to the north of them the whole of the façade of the museum and they can immediately apprehend the configuration of the building: shops, restaurant, education, galleries 1, 2, 3 – they can see where it all is.

The other benefit which will only become apparent when we build the second half of the building is that when you come down the ramp you will look to the right and see to the south a space below the ground level which is nevertheless lit by natural light – the oil tanks, and the space that leads to the oil tanks. There is a space there that will create a connecting art gallery that is the size of the South Duveen gallery at Millbank and of very similar proportions. It will be a very, very dramatic experience to come down this ramp and have these two possibilities on either side of you.

**JH** It also has to do with our idea that when you come into the museum nothing should be lower and nothing should be higher in status. We wanted people to be in front of the north and south façade and to give different areas equal importance. We have three gallery floors that are all of equal height. We also have an opportunity for the curators to have all kinds of art on every floor and to have equal access to the centre.

**NS** That flows from a belief on our part that we shouldn't be establishing hierarchies in the media that are shown in the gallery. What we have tried to do is to create a series of rooms that can be used for any medium.

**JH** You also have to give a clear orientation because it's such a big museum that you would feel lost if somewhere at your back or somewhere up there there's something you don't know about. I think that when you come in almost everyone immediately understands how the building is structured. You can almost physically show that, like in a landscape.

**NS** But then the spatial organisation within the building is also given by certain characteristics as designed by Scott. So for instance the great windows of the north face – because we wanted to have as much natural light as possible in the galleries – start to generate decisions about where the galleries should be and at what level.

**JH** The symmetry of Scott's building is something we had to deal with which I think we all felt sometimes was a bit too heavy. But because the building is so big the symmetry helps. And there are many areas where the symmetry is broken, like the bay windows and the ramp. This balances without destroying the symmetry.

**NS** There was a wish to create a series of rooms in which each would have a definite character but once hung with art it would be the art that came to the fore. Although there are rooms that are breathtakingly beautiful.

**Bankside Power Station under construction in 1951, with the oil tanks visible to the right.**

There are different forms of intrusion, aren't there? It's not just a question of making a room as neutral or as minimal as possible because that can create a tyranny of perfection. There were moments at which we've been trying to recognise that even though we were creating entirely new galleries they lay within Giles Gilbert Scott's building, which had a certain rigour and also an industrial character. For example we had a long debate about what sort of air conditioning we should be using and came to the conclusion that we would use a low-velocity system that involved creating holes in the floor through which the air would rise, and then you and Harry [Gugger] designed a cast iron grille that was a response to the fact that this was originally an industrial building. Or for instance where we were having wooden floors we decided not to have the conventional perfectly smooth or polished gallery floor but have something rougher than that. So the building is not so perfect that as soon as you put a handmade work of art in it it looks too crafted. Works of art that are made by hand don't fit comfortably in buildings that feel as though they are machines.

**JH** I truly think that these are among the most beautiful galleries in the world. It was the most difficult thing to make the galleries very sober, very neutral, very simple, very clear and at the same time to avoid the boring minimalism which is all too perfect. It helps that we didn't have the money to make it all too refined.

**NS** One of the reasons we chose Herzog & de Meuron is that you respond to the particular circumstances of an individual commission, as you find on the grilles, or the handrails or the way the treads work on the stairs. When you first look at those solutions you could almost believe that they were part of the original power station except that they are too refined for Giles Gilbert Scott. You have this sense that the architects have looked at the building and tried to interpret in a contemporary manner a solution that might have been conceived fifty years ago. Not in a retro sense, but in some way they create a bridge between the old and the new.

**JH** Our job is not to say clearly 'this is our intervention' but to create a museum for the twenty-first century where everything works. In some areas it's better not to expose any new materials rather than the old ones because who would be interested in that? We discovered that in many areas using existing materials was just giving better results, whereas in other areas you can clearly see that, for example, the glass light beam is obviously a crisp new element of our time.

We looked at the gallery from the inside and thought what could be better than the existing windows. The strong symmetry was more of a concern than adding a feature, so we did several things with the tower and the light beam. If you look at the building you could see that the symmetry is a fake symmetry and the light beam disbalances it because it doesn't go the full length on one side. And we knew that when we built it the light beam would be such a strong feature, because when you build something in reality it is always more powerful than the drawings. So many architects tend to do more than is needed to be visible in reality.

**Tate Modern, September 2011. The oil tanks, uncovered here during reconstruction work, will be underneath the new extension.**

**NS** An ambition for the Tate was literally to open to a large public a building that had previously been closed. With a very simple gesture Herzog & de Meuron somehow released some of the potential of Scott's box and opened it to the public.

**JH** Those cathedral windows are the best kinds of windows to have. You get light from the side which goes from the floor to the ceiling which opens in this case onto wonderful views of the City of London. Any other opening to the façade would have been stupid.

**NS** It's certainly true that, had it been a product of a single architectural practice – even you and Harry and Pierre [de Meuron] – if it had been a single language throughout as you have in the Pompidou or in the Getty, that single note could become too dominant in terms of then being a receptacle for many different kinds of art. To that extent the incorporation of parts of the old building has been helpful in creating a certain tension. The fact that the building was designed in the mid-twentieth century and the new purpose was to show the art of that century and the next was certainly a nice play for us.

**JH** I always felt the building was older than that. For me, being from outside the country, the fact that it's a brick building and distinctly English makes it very interesting. It couldn't be in Paris or New York. When you talk about the political role of museums it's good that Tate has such an English building, for an international audience, transformed by Swiss architects, and it contains international art.

**NS** It includes the past not in the sense of venerating heritage. It's not a Victorian warehouse where we have simply painted all the iron columns red. It's about using the fabric and giving it new purpose and new life.

Some people, but not artists and not those who can see the subtleties, will regard the galleries as rather conservative spaces. They don't have some of the visual pyrotechnics you get for example in Bilbao, but I challenge anyone to go into some of the double-height spaces and not have their breath taken away. And I hope that they will also be able to look at the art in that context, whereas when you have pyrotechnics the art looks all too insignificant.

It undoubtedly has a very profound physical and psychological impact as you approach it and enter it: the constriction when you come in through the west entrance or in a different way from the north. There's a feeling of compression and then release as you come into the turbine hall.

**JH** But it was never our intention to dwarf people. We hate monumentalism. Monumentalism doesn't mean something that is big but having a one and only goal, which is to impress and to manipulate people.

**NS** One of the things about a museum is that it is a public space but also a place in which people create their own personal space. One of the interesting experiences for a visitor to Tate Modern is the combination of that sense of sharing as you move through the building, but also having your own intimate and individual relationship with a work of art or with a part of the building.

*Abridged from the text first published in 'Building Tate Modern', 2000*

**Left**
**The construction site at night, November 2010, showing the Tanks in the foreground.**

**Right**
**The concourse outside the shop on Level 0.**

First published 2012
by order of the Tate Trustees
by Tate Publishing, a division
of Tate Enterprises Ltd,
Millbank, London SW1P 4RG
www.tate.org.uk/publishing

A catalogue record for this
book is available from the
British Library
ISBN 978 1 84976 065 2

Designed by Esterson Associates
Printed in Spain by Grafos S.A.

Cover: Tate Modern Turbine
Hall, Tate Photography / Andrew
Dunkley and Marcus Leith

MIX
From responsible
sources
FSC
www.fsc.org
FSC® C012329

## Copyright

Joseph Beuys, *Lightning with Stag in its Glare* 1958–85
Tate. Lent from a private collection 2009

Louise Bourgeois, *I Do, I Redo, I Undo* 2000
© the estate of Louise Bourgeois

Louise Bourgeois, *Maman* 1999
Tate. Presented by the artist 2008 © the estate of Louise Bourgeois

Tacita Dean, *FILM* 2011
© the artist

Olafur Eliasson, *The Weather Project* 2003
© the artist

Carsten Höller, *Test Site* 2006
© the artist

Jenny Holzer, *BLUE PURPLE TILT* 2007
ARTIST ROOMS Acquired jointly with the National Galleries of Scotland through The d'Offay Donation with assistance from the National Heritage Memorial Fund and the Art Fund 2008

Anish Kapoor, *Marsyas* 2002
© the artist

Mark Rothko, The Seagram murals
Tate. Presented by the artist through the American Federation of Arts 1969 © Kate Rothko Prizel and Christopher Rothko

Doris Salcedo, *Shibboloth* 2007
© the artist

Do Ho Suh, *Staircase-III* 2012
Tate. Purchased with funds provided by the Asia Pacific Acquisitions Committee 2011
© Do Ho Suh, courtesy Lehmann Maupin Gallery, New York

Ai Weiwei, *Sunflower Seeds* 2010
Tate. Purchased with assistance from Tate International Council, the American Patrons of Tate, the Art Fund, and Stephen and Yana Peel 2012 © the artist

## Photo credits

English Heritage
© Crown Copyright  44

© Chorley Handford  4

© Ian Hay / Above All Images  45

© Hayes Davidson and Herzog & de Meuron  9

Lobster Pictures Ltd 2010  46

© Peter Saville, Hayes Davidson and Herzog & de Meuron  8

Tate Photography / Sam Drake  32

Tate Photography / Andrew Dunkley and Sam Drake  40–1

Tate Photography / Andrew Dunkley and Marcus Leith  2–3, 5, 12–13, 17, 20–1, 22, 25, 26, 27, 28, 29, 30, 33, 34–5, 38–9, 42, 43, 47

Tate Photography / Jo Fernandes  18–19, 36–7

Tate Photography / Marcus Leith  6, 7, 16, 23

Tate Photography / Marcus Leith and Marcella Leith  10–11, 14–15, 24